Savvy

BATHE, BUFF, and Beautify

DIY CRAFTS AND RECIPES
for Natural Body Care

by AUBRE ANDRUS

CAPSTONE PRESS
a capstone imprint

Savvy Books are published by Capstone Press,
1710 Roe Crest Drive, North Mankato, Minnesota 56003
www.mycapstone.com

The Publisher, Author, and any other content providers to this book are not
responsible for any effects that may arise from following the recipes or treatments
and using the products from the recipes in this book.

Library of Congress Cataloging-in-Publication Data
Names: Andrus, Aubre, author.
Title: Bathe, buff, and beautify : DIY crafts and recipes for natural body
care / by Aubre Andrus.
Description: North Mankato, Minnesota : Capstone Press, [2017] | Series:
Savvy. DIY Day Spa | Audience: Age 9-13. | Audience: Grade 4-6. |
Identifiers: LCCN 2016030045| ISBN 9781515734468 (library binding) |
ISBN 9781515734505 (eBook PDF)
Subjects: LCSH: Baths—Health aspects—Juvenile literature. |
Health—Juvenile literature. | Grooming—Juvenile literature. |
Handicraft—Juvenile literature.
Classification: LCC RA780 .A53 2017 | DDC 615.3/6—dc23
LC record available at https://lccn.loc.gov/2016030045

Editor: Eliza Leahy
Designer: Tracy McCabe
Creative Director: Heather Kindseth
Production Specialist: Katy LaVigne

Image Credits: Photographs by Capstone Studio: Karon Dubke,
photographer; Sarah Schuette, photo stylist; Marcy Morin,
studio scheduler; Author photo by Ariel Andrus

Printed in the United States of America.
042017   010421R

TABLE OF CONTENTS

INTRODUCTION

Creating a spa experience at home is easier than you might think. Believe it or not, you'll find a lot of what you need in the kitchen! The recipes in this book aren't much different from traditional recipes (such as cupcakes, cookies, and cake), but these recipes aren't meant to be eaten. Instead of soothing your hunger, these recipes soothe your body!

Sensitive skin? There's a calming recipe for you. Itchy, dry skin? There's an exfoliating and moisturizing product that can help. There's even a recipe for a lavender-scented lotion that will help you get your beauty rest. After all, one of the best parts about a spa experience is the delicious scents, so we added some essential oils to make your DIY spa experience as relaxing as the real thing.

Flip through these pages to find your favorites in the same way you'd flip through a cookbook. There's no wrong or right place to start. There's a homemade spa product for everyone, from salves to scrubs to sprays to soaks.

Enjoy these products alone, give them as gifts, or invite some friends over for a spa party.

IT'S TIME TO PAMPER YOURSELF!

SPECIALTY INGREDIENTS

Some of the recipes in this book call for simple ingredients that you may already have in your kitchen, such as baking soda, olive oil, or vanilla extract. But there are some specialty ingredients that you likely won't find at home.

Luckily, they can be found at health food stores or organic grocery stores near the spices, pharmacy, or beauty aisles. You can also find them online. Here are some of those ingredients and the reasons you need them in your recipes.

beeswax pastilles

shea butter

Epsom salts

Beeswax – Beeswax helps firm balms and creams. These recipes call for grated beeswax, which can be made by using a cheese grater on a bar of pure beeswax. Or you could buy beeswax pastilles, which are small granules or pellets.

Citric Acid – Citric acid is a powder that helps create a "fizz" in bath and shower products. It can be found in the canning or bulk spice aisle in health food stores.

Coconut Oil – Coconut oil moisturizes your skin and hair.

Distilled Water – Distilled water has been boiled to remove impurities, and it will help your ingredients last longer. It can be found at grocery stores.

Epsom Salts – Epsom salts soothe aching muscles and relieve itching from dry skin and insect bites.

Jojoba Oil – Jojoba oil is soothing when applied to irritated skin, from acne to sunburn.

Sea Salt – The rough texture of sea salt helps exfoliate skin while naturally detoxifying.

Shea Butter – Shea butter moisturizes and balances skin without clogging pores. It can even help heal cuts and scrapes.

Vegetable Glycerin – Vegetable glycerin naturally attracts moisture when applied to skin.

Witch Hazel – Witch hazel soothes itchy or irritated skin, including acne and foot infections. It can also tighten and moisturize skin.

ESSENTIAL OILS

Many of the recipes in this book call for essential oils. Essential oils are used for aromatherapy (they smell lovely and can make you feel great) and for health benefits for your hair, skin, and body.

They can be found at health food stores, organic grocery stores, or online. Here are the essential oils used in this book and the reasons you might use them in your recipes.

Lavender
Lavender is probably the most popular essential oil. It can soothe skin and possibly help fight acne. It has a floral aroma that can help you fall asleep.

Roman Chamomile
Roman chamomile essential oil soothes skin and has a calming aroma that can help you wind down and clear your sinuses.

Lemon*
Lemon essential oil is antibacterial. It can prevent infection when applied to the skin. Its citrus aroma is energizing.

Orange*

Orange essential oil is a natural cleanser and deodorizer, and it can help heal skin. Like lemon, its citrus aroma is energizing.

Peppermint

Peppermint essential oil has a cooling effect. It can relieve muscle pain and has an invigorating aroma that can make you feel alert.

Tea Tree

Tea tree oil fights bacteria, fungi, and viruses, so it can help treat athlete's foot, acne, and more when applied to the skin.

Be careful! Don't allow any undiluted essential oil to get on your skin or in your eyes or mouth. Recipes from this book containing essential oils should not be used on children under age 6, and for older children, an adult's help is recommended.

*Lemon and orange essential oils could be phototoxic, which means they can make your skin extra-sensitive to the sun. Don't apply citrus essential oils to bare skin before going outside. And always wear sunscreen!

MEASURING YOUR INGREDIENTS

Essential oils are very potent and must be diluted with distilled water or a carrier oil, such as coconut oil, jojoba oil, or olive oil. It might not seem like you're using a lot, but a little goes a long way!

The recipes in this book dilute the essential oil to about 1 percent. That means some recipes require only a few drops. We measure essential oils by the drop in this book because it's hard to measure any other way. (There are 20 drops in 1 milliliter, and ¼ teaspoon is a little more than 1 milliliter.) There are very few recipes that will require more than ¼ teaspoon of essential oil.

coconut oil

jojoba oil

olive oil

HOW TO SAFELY MELT BUTTER AND OIL

Shea butter is a soft solid that must be melted for many recipes in this book. A double boiler is best for melting oils and butters, but you can also microwave them at 50 percent power in 30-second increments, stirring in between, until the solid is almost all the way melted. Stir to complete the melting process. You don't want to overheat the oils or butters.

Coconut oil is also used often in this book. Whether your coconut oil is a solid or a liquid depends on where you live, what time of year it is, and the air temperature. To solidify it, place it in the refrigerator until it hardens. To liquefy it, heat it in a microwave-safe bowl in 10-second increments at 50 percent power, stirring in between, until the solid is almost all the way melted.

It's best to heat the solids in a microwave-safe bowl with a pourable spout and a handle, such as a glass Pyrex measuring cup. Be sure to always wear an oven mitt when removing a hot bowl from the microwave.

HOW TO SAFELY STORE YOUR PRODUCTS

It's best to use glass containers, not plastic, to store any recipe that contains essential oils, because the essential oils can deteriorate plastic over time. All of the recipes in this book make small batches since they are natural and don't contain preservatives.

Unless indicated otherwise, the finished products should be stored in a cool, dry place and should be used within two to four weeks. Never use a recipe if it looks like it has grown mold, if it has changed colors, or if it begins to smell bad.

ALLERGIES

Some people have skin sensitivities and allergies. Check with your doctor or dermatologist before using any of these recipes.

CLEAN UP

Many of the recipes in this book use oils and butters, which might feel greasy. To clean up, wipe your hands and any used dishes with a dry paper towel first, then use soap and water to wash. When using recipes in the bathtub, such as sugar scrubs, wipe the floor clean with a dry towel afterward. Oils and butters can make surfaces slippery and unsafe.

WHERE TO FIND PACKAGING FOR YOUR PRODUCTS

It's important to use brand new containers to store your products. It will help prevent mold from growing. Here's where you can buy containers that are perfect for the recipes in this book:

• reusable 2-ounce (59-milliliter) glass bottles or 4-ounce (118-mL) glass containers can be found in the essential oil aisle at health food stores

• reusable 2-ounce (59-mL) plastic spray bottles or 3-ounce (89-mL) plastic squeeze bottles can be found in the travel section of grocery or convenience stores

• reusable 4-ounce (118-mL) spice tins or empty spice jars can be found in the bulk spice aisle in grocery stores or health food stores

• half-pint glass jars can be found in the jam or canning aisle in grocery stores or health food stores

• round plastic containers with screw-top lids can be found in the jewelry or bead storage aisle at craft stores or in the travel aisle of department stores

Shower Pouf

You will need:

1 yard (90 centimeters) of 72-inch
    (183-cm) wide nylon netting
8-inch (20-cm) length ofcording
2 yards (183 cm) of dental floss
needle
safety pins
scissors

Scrub-a-dub-dub! These shower poufs are quick and simple to make, and they make great gifts too. Use a different color netting in the center to make an extra pretty pouf, or add more layers for an extra fluffy version.

DIRECTIONS:

Cut the nylon netting into 3 strips that each measure 6 x 72 inches (15 x 183 cm). Stack the layers, then secure stacks in place at top, bottom, and center with safety pins. Thread the needle, then knot end of floss to safety pin at bottom. Starting at bottom center, sew a long running stitch, about 1 inch (2.5 cm) in length. Repeat along entire length of netting.

Remove safety pins from fabric, then grab each end of floss. Push netting toward center. Tie ends of floss tightly in a double knot. The netting should now form a sphere. Trim ends. Secure a loop of cording through the center and finish with a knot.

Vanilla Honey Shower Scrub

You will need:

1 cup (240 mL) white sugar
¼ cup (60 mL) olive oil
2 tbsp (30 mL) honey
½ tsp (2.5 mL) vanilla extract

sugar

Exfoliating sugar scrubs are great for your skin. While showering, scoop a small amount into your hands. Rub it into your skin, then rinse well. Not only will you feel re-energized, but your shower will smell delicious!

Be careful! Oils and butters can make bathtub surfaces slippery. A non-slip bath mat may help. Wipe bathtub floor with a dry towel when finished.

DIRECTIONS:

Mix all ingredients in a small bowl. Store in a lidded glass container.
Makes about 1 cup (240 mL). Store in a cool, dry place.

Secret Solid Perfume

You will need:

2 tbsp (30 mL) grated beeswax or beeswax pastilles
2 tsp (10 mL) jojoba oil
10 drops Roman chamomile essential oil
4 drops orange essential oil
10 drops lavender essential oil

This solid perfume makes a great gift and is perfect for girls on the go. Reuse a miniature mint tin, a small jam jar, or even a jewelry locket and keep it in your bag or pocket. No one will know what's really inside!

beeswax pastilles

DIRECTIONS:

Scoop beeswax into a microwave-safe bowl with a pourable spout. Microwave in 30-second increments at 50 percent power, stirring each time, until it mostly liquefies. Remove bowl with an oven mitt and stir until clear, not cloudy. Add jojoba oil and essential oils and stir. Immediately pour into container of your choice. Let harden at room temperature. This recipe makes about 1 tablespoon (15 mL). Store in a cool, dry place.

Tub Teas

These bags of tub tea are so simple to make and use. Store each organza bag in a reusable zip-top bag in case they leak a bit—it's okay if they do! To use, fill bathtub with warm water, then place organza bag directly in water and let it soak for the duration of your bath. Remove the organza bag when done and dispose of the bag in the garbage.

Calming Tub Tea

This fragrance-free mix is perfect for sensitive skin.

You will need:

3 x 4 inch (7.5 x 10 cm)
  organza bag
½ cup (120 mL) oats
½ cup (120 mL) powdered milk
¼ cup (60 mL) Epsom salts
1 tsp (5 mL) baking soda

powdered milk

Re-energizing Tub Tea

A wake-me-up blend that energizes tired muscles.

You will need:

3 x 4 inch (7.5 x 10 cm) organza bag
½ cup (120 mL) oats
½ cup (120 mL) Epsom salts
¼ cup (60 mL) coarse sea salt
5 drops peppermint essential oil
10 drops lemon essential oil
10 drops orange essential oil

DIRECTIONS:

Blend oats in a food processor or blender. Mix all ingredients in a bowl with a pourable spout. Pour into organza bag and tie in a knot. Makes 1 bag.

Cinnamon Vanilla Whipped Body Butter

This whipped body butter looks like luxurious lotion, and it will melt in your hands. Your skin will feel silky smooth, will look like it's glowing, and will smell good too! Massage this into your skin before bed, so the lotion can work its magic all night. Remember, a little goes a long way.

DIRECTIONS:

Scoop shea butter into a microwave-safe mixing bowl. Microwave in 30-second increments at 50 percent power, stirring each time, until it mostly liquefies. Remove bowl with an oven mitt. Stir in coconut oil until clear, not cloudy. Add jojoba oil and stir.

To turn the mixture into cream, cover bowl with plastic wrap and let cool in refrigerator until the texture resembles softened butter (this step should take no longer than an hour). If mixture fully hardens, remove from refrigerator and let it warm on the counter. Add cinnamon and vanilla, then whip with a hand mixer on low speed for 3-5 minutes or until the color brightens and peaks form.

When desired consistency is reached, scoop into lidded glass jar with a spoon. Makes about 1 cup (240 mL). Store in a cool, dry place.

Natural Shaving Cream

You will need:

⅓ cup (80 mL) shea butter
⅓ cup (80 mL) coconut oil
2 tbsp (30 mL) olive oil

Make your own nourishing and natural lotion that protects your skin while you shave. This cream is thick and may clog your razor blade. Rinse blade under water after every few strokes. Clean the razor after each use by soaking it in a cup with dish soap and hot water, then scrubbing it clean with an old toothbrush.

shea butter

Be careful! Oils and butters can make bathtub surfaces slippery. A non-slip bath mat may help. Wipe bathtub floor with a dry towel when finished.

DIRECTIONS:

Scoop shea butter into a microwave-safe mixing bowl. Microwave in 30-second increments at 50 percent power, stirring each time, until it mostly liquefies. Remove bowl with an oven mitt. Stir in coconut oil until clear, not cloudy. Add olive oil and stir.

To turn the mixture into cream, cover bowl with plastic wrap and let cool in refrigerator until the texture resembles softened butter (this step should take no longer than an hour). If mixture fully hardens, remove from refrigerator and let it warm on the counter. Whip with a hand mixer on low speed for 3-5 minutes or until the color brightens and peaks form.

When desired consistency is reached, scoop into jar with spatula. Makes about 1 cup (240 mL). Store in a cool, dry place.

Sweet Dreams Cream

You will need:

1 cup (240 mL) coconut oil
15 drops lavender essential oil
25 drops Roman chamomile
    essential oil

Coconut oil is great for your skin. This whipped version makes it even easier to use. You can rub this sleep salve just about anywhere: your hands, your feet, even your temples. The lavender and chamomile will help lull you to dreamland. Remember, a little goes a long way.

DIRECTIONS:

Scoop the coconut oil into a mixing bowl. Does it look and feel like softened butter? Then it's ready to go! (If it's liquid, cover bowl with plastic wrap and let harden in refrigerator until the texture resembles softened butter. This step should take no longer than an hour.) Add essential oil, then whip with a hand mixer on low speed for 3-5 minutes or until the color brightens and peaks form.

When desired consistency is reached, scoop into jar with spatula. Depending on how much the ingredients are whipped, this recipe makes about enough to fill a 4-ounce (118-mL) jar. Store in a cool, dry place.

Bathing Beauty Melts

You will need:

1 cup (240 mL) shea butter
1 tbsp (15 mL) coconut oil
2 tbsp (30 mL) Epsom salts
¼ cup (60 mL) baking soda
10 drops lavender essential oil (optional)
5 drops Roman chamomile essential oil (optional)
1 tbsp (15 mL) pink edible glitter (optional)
silicone treat molds

Transform your bathtub into a spa-like soak when you drop one of these bath melts inside. This recipe may be called "bathing beauty," but it will help lull you into "sleeping beauty" mode. Chamomile and lavender have a calming effect for the perfect bedtime mix, but these beauty melts are great without essential oils too.

Epsom salts

Be careful! Oils and butters can make bathtub surfaces slippery. A non-slip bath mat may help. Wipe bathtub floor with a dry towel when finished.

DIRECTIONS:

Melt the shea butter in 30-second increments at 50 percent power in a microwave-safe bowl with a pourable spout. Carefully remove from microwave with oven mitt. Stir in coconut oil until melted.

Stir in Epsom salts, baking soda, essential oils, and shimmer dust. Pour mixture into silicone treat molds and let harden at room temperature. Makes 5-6 medium-sized bath melts. Store individually in a cool, dry place.

Spa Towel Wrap

You will need:

bath towel
safety pin
12 inches (30 cm) of Velcro tape,
   ¾ inch (2 cm) in width
permanent fabric glue
marker or masking tape
washcloth of a different color (optional)

It's the perfect blend between a towel and a robe! With a little bit of Velcro, this wrap stays in place, which means you can dry off hands free.

Optional: Cut shapes from a washcloth of a different color and glue them to the outside of the towel wrap as decoration. Let dry overnight.

DIRECTIONS:

With the top corner in each hand, hold a towel open and centered behind you. Wrap the left edge around the front of your body until it reaches your right armpit.

Make an X with a marker or masking tape on the corner nearest your right armpit and again near your left armpit.

Now wrap the right edge around the front of your body so it reaches your left armpit. Fold the excess material inward and pin it in place.

Make two Xs on on the inside of the outer layer of the towel by simply mirroring the Xs you already made.

Remove the towel from your body and lay it flat on the ground with excess material facing up. Run a length of glue along the inside edges of excess material and press firmly. Remove safety pin.

Cut four 3-inch (7.5-cm) pieces of Velcro tape (two pieces of each kind). Glue the Velcro strips with scratchy sides to the Xs on this side of the towel. Flip over the towel, then glue the Velcro strips with fuzzy sides to the Xs. Let dry overnight.

Bath Salts

Soak your cares away. These bath salts turn any regular tub into a soothing experience. To use, dissolve bath salts into warm water, then soak inside the tub for 20 minutes. The salts in this recipe have great detoxifying benefits and can help relieve aches and pains. Choose the lavender version for its calming properties that relax your mind and your muscles, or pick peppermint for an invigorating soak.

Epsom salts

sea salt

Lovely Lavender Bath Salts

You will need:

1 cup (240 mL) sea salt
1 cup (240 mL) Epsom salts
10 drops lavender essential oil
2-3 drops purple food
   coloring (optional)

Peppermint Bath Salts

You will need:

1 cup (240 mL) sea salt
1 cup (240 mL) Epsom salts
10 drops peppermint essential oil
2-3 drops green food coloring
   (optional)

DIRECTIONS:

Pour the salts into a lidded glass container. Add essential oil, then food coloring.
Stir all ingredients together. Makes 2 cups (480 mL) or enough for two soaks.
Store extra for up to two weeks in a cool, dry place.

Mocha Salt Scrub

You will need:

- ½ cup (120 mL) coarse sea salt
- ¼ cup (60 mL) ground coffee
- ¼ cup (60 mL) olive oil
- 1 tbsp (15 mL) cocoa powder
- ½ tsp (2.5 mL) vanilla extract

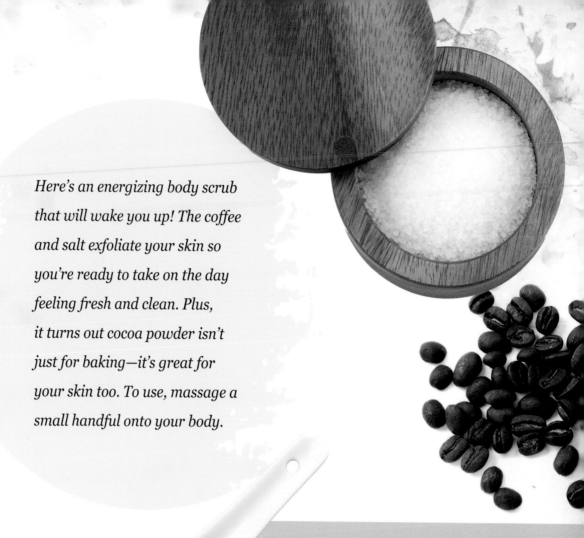

Here's an energizing body scrub that will wake you up! The coffee and salt exfoliate your skin so you're ready to take on the day feeling fresh and clean. Plus, it turns out cocoa powder isn't just for baking—it's great for your skin too. To use, massage a small handful onto your body.

Be careful! Oils and butters can make bathtub surfaces slippery. A non-slip bath mat may help. Wipe bathtub floor with a dry towel when finished.

DIRECTIONS:

Mix all ingredients in a bowl. Stir together, then scoop into a lidded jar. Makes about 1 cup (240 mL). Store in a cool, dry place.

Shower Steamers

Aromatherapy is the use of essential oils in bath products to help balance mind, body, and spirit. These shower steamers smell great, thanks to a blend of essential oils that release into the air as you shower. To use, wet a steamer in your shower and place it on a ledge. Depending on the size of your steamers, you may want to use more than one at a time.

Good Night Shower Steamers

This is a relaxing blend that calms your mind and your body.

You will need:

1 cup (240 mL) baking soda
½ cup (120 mL) citric acid
1 tbsp (15 mL) witch hazel in spray bottle
5 drops lavender essential oil
10 drops Roman chamomile essential oil
5 drops orange essential oil
silicone mold
rubber gloves

Good Morning Shower Steamers

A happy, energizing mix to wake you up and put a smile on your face.

You will need:

1 cup (240 mL) baking soda
½ cup (120 mL) citric acid
1 tbsp (15 mL) witch hazel in spray bottle
5 drops peppermint essential oil
10 drops lemon essential oil
10 drops orange essential oil
silicone mold
rubber gloves

Be careful! Wear gloves when making this recipe. Citric acid could irritate your skin or eyes.

Tip: If the scent wears off, apply a few drops of essential oil directly to each shower steamer before using.

DIRECTIONS:

In a large bowl, combine the baking soda and citric acid. Stir until all lumps are removed. Add essential oils and stir. Spritz mixture with 5-10 sprays of witch hazel, then mix with your hands (don't forget the gloves!).

Continue until mixture is slightly damp, but not wet enough to form a ball. Use as little witch hazel as possible, otherwise the shower steamers will expand as they dry.

When the mixture reaches the desired texture, press it firmly into silicone molds. Let dry overnight. Remove carefully from molds, then store in a resealable plastic bag or glass jar. Makes about 5 small shower steamers.

Luxurious Lotion Bars

You will need:

- ½ cup (120 mL) coconut oil
- ½ cup (120 mL) shea butter
- ½ cup (120 mL) grated beeswax or beeswax pastilles
- 20 drops Roman chamomile essential oil (optional)
- silicone treat mold

These lotion bars are great for traveling. Although they're solid, the warmth from your hands allows them to easily melt into a luxurious cream exactly when you need it. They make great gifts too!

DIRECTIONS:

Scoop shea butter and beeswax into a microwave-safe bowl with a pourable spout. Microwave in 30-second increments at 50 percent power, stirring each time, until mixture mostly liquefies. Remove bowl with an oven mitt. Stir in coconut oil until clear, not cloudy. Let cool slightly, then add essential oil.

Using an oven mitt, carefully pour liquid into silicone molds. Let harden overnight at room temperature, then remove carefully from mold. Store in an airtight container in a cool, dry place.

Bugs-Be-Gone Spray

You will need:

- 3 tbsp (45 mL) witch hazel
- 2 tbsp (30 mL) distilled water
- ½ tsp (2.5 mL) vegetable glycerin
- 15 drops tea tree essential oil
- 5 drops lavender essential oil

Keep the bugs at bay with a natural spray. Tea tree oil and lavender are said to help repel mosquitoes, while witch hazel can reduce that itchy feeling that accompanies a nasty bite. To use, spritz onto exposed skin before going outside. Avoid contact with your eyes.

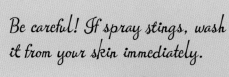

Be careful! If spray stings, wash it from your skin immediately.

DIRECTIONS:

Mix ingredients in a glass bowl with a pourable spout.
Pour into a 2-ounce (59-mL) spray bottle.

DIY Deodorant

You can whip up this natural alternative at home. This is a deodorant, so it will prevent body odor. However, it is not an antiperspirant, so it won't prevent sweating. Depending on what you believe, that may be a good thing; some people argue that sweating is good for your body.

You will need:

½ cup (120 mL) coconut oil
¼ cup (60 mL) cornstarch
¼ cup (60 mL) baking soda
15 drops tea tree essential oil

DIRECTIONS:

Scoop coconut oil into a microwave-safe bowl with pourable spout. Microwave in 10-second increments at 50 percent power, stirring each time, until it mostly liquefies. Remove bowl with oven mitt and stir until clear, not cloudy. Let cool slightly, then stir in additional ingredients.

Create a tight seal at the bottom of an empty deodorant tube by screwing canister to its lowest setting. (Reuse a deodorant tube or buy an empty deodorant tube at an online specialty shop.) Wearing an oven mitt to protect your hand, hold the deodorant tube over a garbage can. Then carefully pour liquid into empty tube until full. Place cap on top and keep in refrigerator overnight until liquid solidifies.

DIY Deodorant for Sensitive Skin

If the above recipe is too harsh on your skin, it may be because of the baking soda. This recipe lessens the baking soda and replaces it with soothing shea butter, which should help alleviate some skin sensitivities.

You will need:

⅓ cup (80 mL) coconut oil
⅓ cup (80 mL) grated beeswax or beeswax pastilles
⅓ cup (80 mL) cornstarch
3 tbsp (45 mL) shea butter
2 tbsp (30 mL) baking soda
15 drops tea tree essential oil

DIRECTIONS:

Scoop beeswax and shea butter into a microwave-safe bowl with pourable spout. Microwave in 30-second increments at 50 percent power, stirring each time, until it mostly liquefies. Remove bowl with an oven mitt. Stir in coconut oil until clear, not cloudy. Let cool slightly, then stir in additional ingredients.

Create a tight seal at the bottom of an empty deodorant tube by screwing canister to its lowest setting. (Reuse a deodorant tube or buy an empty deodorant tube at an online specialty shop.) Wearing an oven mitt to protect your hand, hold the deodorant tube over a garbage can. Then carefully pour liquid into empty tube until full. Place cap on top and keep in refrigerator overnight until liquid solidifies.

Gift Wrap: Nail Polish Marbling

You will need:

4 bottles of nail polish
grosgrain or satin ribbon of any width or length
paper gift tags
disposable plastic food container or bowl
water
toothpick
parchment paper

Give some of your favorite beauty products to your friends as gifts! Decorating ribbons and tags with a beautiful marbling effect is a lot easier than it looks. A mix of nail polish and water is the perfect paint to brighten up plain wrapping. Four different bold or metallic jewel tones mix together best. As soon as the nail polish hits the water, it will begin to dry, so be sure to set up your supplies ahead of time and work fast.

Tip: Make your own paper gift tags! Trace the bottom of a jar or glass onto a piece of card stock, then cut out the circle. Use as is or add a hole at the top center with a hole punch. Loop ribbon through the hole.

DIRECTIONS:

Line your surface with parchment paper. It will act as a space for your finished pieces to dry and will protect the surface from any spills. Now fill a shallow disposable plastic food container with an inch of water. Pour a few drops of each color of nail polish into the bowl. Swirl colors with a toothpick.

Now grab each end of a ribbon length and set it along the surface of the water (keep the ends of the ribbon and your fingers out of the water). The nail polish pattern will imprint onto the ribbon like a stamp. Remove ribbon and place on the parchment paper to dry. Repeat with more ribbon or gift tags. For gift tags, immerse only half the tag in the mixture to avoid getting your hands wet.

To clean up, run a toothpick through the water to gather remaining nail polish (it will clump together). Throw it away. Pour water carefully down the sink, then dispose of the container or save it for a future marbling craft.

CONGRATS TO YOU!

You've made all-natural recipes that beautify your mind and body. Which one was your favorite? The calming or the rejuvenating? The scrubbing or the soothing?

It's important to pamper yourself every week—if not every day. Taking even just five minutes to relax with one of your favorite recipes can relieve stress, calm your nerves, and help you find focus.

Once you've spoiled yourself, don't forget to share the love by giving away these beauty products as gifts. Or throw a party and pamper your guests with spa-like treatments.

It's all about feeling beautiful in the skin you're in. When you feel beautiful, you look beautiful!

READ MORE

Anton, Carrie. *Spa-mazing!: Discover your own way to relax and pamper yourself with activities, quizzes, crafts-and more!* Truly Me. Middleton, Wis.: American Girl, 2016.

Scheunemann, Pam. *Cool Stuff for Bath & Beauty: Creative Handmade Projects for Kids.* Cool Stuff. Minneapolis: Abdo Publishing, 2012.

Skelley, Paula and **Nancy Loewen**. *Tangles, Growth Spurts, and Being You: Questions and Answers About Growing Up.* Girl Talk. North Mankato, Minn.: Capstone Press, 2015.

Titles in this set:

 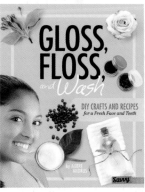 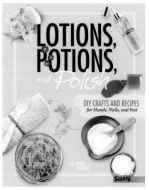 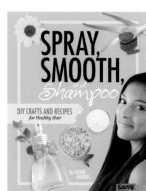

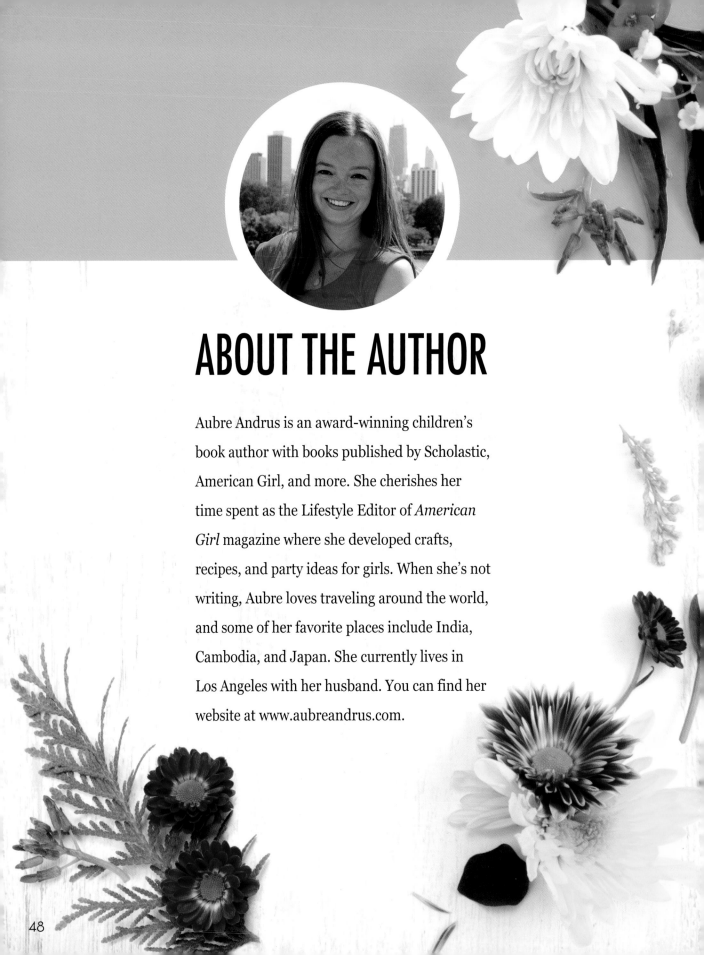

ABOUT THE AUTHOR

Aubre Andrus is an award-winning children's book author with books published by Scholastic, American Girl, and more. She cherishes her time spent as the Lifestyle Editor of *American Girl* magazine where she developed crafts, recipes, and party ideas for girls. When she's not writing, Aubre loves traveling around the world, and some of her favorite places include India, Cambodia, and Japan. She currently lives in Los Angeles with her husband. You can find her website at www.aubreandrus.com.